GLOWING IN THE SHADOWS

BY
AIYSHA SWALLOWGREN

© 2024 Aiysha Swallowgren

All rights reserved. No part of this publication may be reproduced, distributed, or transmitted in any form without the express written permission of the publisher, except in the case of brief quotations embodied in critical reviews and certain other noncommercial uses permitted by copyright law.

ISBN 979-8-9878596-2-9
First Printing February 2024
Printed in United States of America

Contents

Affirming / 5, Alone / 6, Angel of Poetry / 7, Anxiety / 8, Art / 9,
Baring / 10, Best / 11, Better Man / 12, Biggest Pervert / 13, Blossom / 14,
Brushing / 15, Buckle / 16, Caring / 17, Charming / 18, Compose / 19,
Connected / 20, Consciousness / 21, Consistency / 22, Consistently / 23,
Copy / 24, Corruption / 25, Cruel / 26, Dare / 27,
Darkness in the Light / 28, Degrade / 29, Destroy / 30, Destroying / 31,
Destruction / 32, Disaster / 33, Distracted / 34, Done / 35, Dreaming / 36,
Elegant / 37, Enchanted / 38, Especially / 39, Esteem / 40, Exciting / 41,
Expanding / 42, Express / 43, Favorite / 44, Favorite Flower / 45,
Filthy Slave / 46, Fire / 47, First / 48, Fit / 49, Flesh / 50, Forgotten / 51,
Four / 52, Gardening / 53, Gentle / 54, Handcuffed / 55, In Heat / 56,
Intense / 57, Invest / 58, Jizz Junkie / 59, Kindling / 60, King / 61,
Kiss Here / 62, Late / 63, Learning / 64, Leaving / 65, Liberate / 66,
Liberating / 67, Liberation / 68, Little Volcano / 69, Loves More / 70,
Maid / 71, Merry / 72, Mi Amor / 73, Mind / 74, Missing / 75, Nasty / 76,
Nerdy / 77, Nobility / 78, Noble / 79, Nurturing / 80, Obsessed / 81,
Overflowing / 82, Overwhelming / 83, Picnic / 84, Pink Hints / 85,
Piss / 86, Potential / 87, Power / 88, Practicing / 89, Prescribing / 90,
Professor / 91, Protected / 92, Prowess / 93, Queen / 94, Real Cat / 95,
Reassured / 96, Reconnect / 97, Red / 98, Red Bottom / 99,
Refreshing / 100, Replaceable / 101, Respect / 102, Scolding / 103,
Sculpting / 104, Shower / 105, Sinner / 106, Sore / 107, Stir / 108,
Stray / 109, Submit / 110, Sunset / 111, Supermam / 112, Sweetie / 113,
Sweetly Divine / 114, Teaming / 115, Thought / 116, Toilet / 117,
Too Sweet / 118, Training / 119, Tranquility / 120, Tree / 121,
Trimming / 122, Trusting / 123, Two Men / 124, Understanding / 125,
Very New / 126, Vibrating / 127, Waiting / 128, Wake / 129,
Wallpaper / 130, Writer / 131

Affirming

Words of light permeated her space, positive life affirming
Things reminding her that we're constantly learning
Whispering things that create a positive yearning
I came to share light and I'm over here serving
Her soul the most decadent things I'm affirming
That there have been chapters of your life disturbing
I encourage total triumph, start converting
All negativity into the fire I'm stirring
Up her deepest, mist intense learning
Let me light a fire that will never stop burning
They tried dampening your spirit, tried hurting
You deeply but they failed now what's occurring
Is the champion phoenix is immersing
Herself in healing with my loving, sweet wording
She was the very best, she was most deserving
I remind her of her worthiness, the ultimate reassuring
Powerfully I stand in my truth, I'm concerning
Myself with melting everything my fire is purging
All negativity what remains is uniquely birthing
She was inspired to create art with his encouraging
I've always believed in you tremendously, always affirming

Alone

I like being on her mind late at night she's alone
Stirring up her desires like a cyclone
Leading her deeper into temptation, the vast unknown
Whispering allow me to give you a new moan
Something to get you relaxed when alone
She's my queen and I'm worshipping her throne
My mouth expertly playing her polished saxophone
Making beautiful jazz, licking her collarbone
Nothing warms her like when her mind gets blown
She couldn't help but letting out a moan
Reading the raciest things on her phone
Her passion and appetite has really grown
She loved being told and shown
How much I can expand her erogenous zone
She is my treasure, my most valuable gemstone
We both know what she's doing when reading this alone

Angel of Poetry

She inspires me to be an angel of poetry
She said love me solely
On my potential and I experience such a rosary
You make roses bloom, you're an angel poetry
When I speak to her softly and slowly
She felt intense energy he solely
Wants to bring out the most holy
Parts of her he soulfully
Whispered you bring out the angel of poetry

Anxiety

He came into her world of anxiety
He listened a lot, quietly
He took away her away entirely
He did it very hotly and nicely
Soon her memories of anxiety
Would be just that he set her free
Together they made an art diary
They were an asset to society
When relaxed and free from anxiety

Art

She hung my poems on her wall as art
She said they're quite beautiful I'll start
Cheering her on to make priceless art
When I met you I thought what an incredible heart
Let me be your battery and jumpstart
Your mood by being the biggest sweetheart
I reflect back your light which becomes art
What I enjoy most about your company is how smart
You are, oh yeah and she makes dazzling, stunning art
Mentally together, physically apart
What do I admire most of Jess I don't know where to start

Baring

I started wondering about soul baring
If I said you make it easy to start sharing
That you create safety to encourage my most daring
Parts you care deeply, you're very caring
That's why is so natural to start baring
My soul we're both quite sensitive is a good pairing
You enjoy how I am unable to quit staring
At you no matter what you're wearing
I want to share warmth making you start swearing
Love is in actions love starts repairing
Between us it's always safe vulnerably baring.

Best

She flattered me saying I'm the erotica best
I'm massaging your scalp, you're so stressed
I'm tying your mind up, it's under arrest
Don't fall in love dear, become obsessed
About a man more focused on your mind than your chest
Now that you're handcuffed and gagged you can't protest
I'm hitting you so roughly, I start to suggest
That I'm going to make your body shake like you're possessed
You win first prize in any beauty contest
Your makeup was nice but I really messed
It up making you redefine the word blessed
I want to keep you speechless and impressed
Dear you always bring out my erotic best

Better Man

I wanted you to know you make me want to be a better man
When it comes to inspiration there's nothing better than
You I'm the atomic bomb and you're my Japan
You give the sun a warm suntan
Would you hold it against me if I'm your biggest fan
I'm a fan of those that make me be a better man
I'm not an angel, I have little wingspan
You're a cold stick of butter and I a flying pan
You always knew I was far from a clergyman
It's not the American Revolution and I'm no minuteman
In short you Jane, me Tarzan
You make things complicated, you make me a better man
You're the bomb, more than Afghanistan
I'm no hero, you're my kryptonite but I'm not Superman
Am I ever on your radar, do I warrant your attention span
You have a cat, maybe you're my Catwoman
I won't ghost you ever, but I'm batty like Batman
In spite of everything you inspire me to be a better man

Biggest Pervert

She desired to be in the mind of the biggest pervert
She craved his large firm hands up her skirt
He treated her like a dog, treated like dirt
He had so many ideas she loved how he hurt
Her in new and creative ways her biggest pervert
Slapped her roughly and ripped her shirt
Hands in her mouth she would happily insert
All of them he was dominant and would assert
His large power she loved when the biggest pervert
Would smother her his fat body made her alert
She would pass out from the force he would exert
From a queen to a dirty slut he was able to convert
Her he collected his sperm and made her yogurt
She craved his delicious perverted dessert
She eagerly swallowed the essence of the biggest pervert

Blossom

What's the best way to make her butterfly blossom
It's to make her belly laugh which is no problem
He made her pleasure increase she will become
More and more open letting her flower blossom
I whispered about how to make her stress less from
The inside she always had time to succumb
To feeling great maybe even as great as her bum
Creating sensations in her body, she felt so young
Imagining all the ways to please her using my tongue
I'm all about helping her achieve her outcome
Making her glow, making her feel awesome
I'm watching her glowing butterfly blossom

Brushing

After bathing her in oils I start brushing
Her beautiful hair there's nothing
She enjoys more than a man that isn't rushing
I enjoy whispering things that get her blushing
The slower and more polite I become, the more cussing
Comes out of her mouth, my hands lightly brushing
Her neck and shoulders she's becoming
Totally undone, her nipples start puffing
Out, prolonged foreplay makes her want disgusting
Things done to her I'm roughly thrusting
Inside her mind like a bee I'm wildly buzzing
In her flower covered in her pollen she's huffing
I am an artist and she's my canvas expertly brushing
Her excited body until she starts gushing
I'm taking her new places, she's trusting
Me to give her the most unique loving
Driving her wild I start handcuffing
Her she's begging me to start roughing
Her up, I take my large hands and start stuffing
My canvas wildly with creative, intense brushing

Buckle

I know how to make her leak and her hips buckle
She's such a party girl it makes me chuckle
She loves my large hands how my muscle
Touches her roughly it gives her double
Pleasure when I use my belt, especially the buckle
Looking at me expose her as I suckle
Her hot breasts she's making a pleasure puddle
I like making her lose control when she struggle
I'm making it so creamy blowing her bubble
She feels my rocket, I'm her space shuttle
I play very roughly then start to cuddle
She loves when I force her to guzzle
My cum and invite others to huddle
Over watching as her inner whore starts to buckle
She loves it naughty and I'm the definition of trouble

Caring

I met the loveliest nurse, so caring
I can't take my eyes off her, I'm staring
She loves my pouts, my glaring
We raise each other up, we are daring
To make unique love, there's no comparing
Her love to anyone else, she's most caring
Sometimes she is intense and starts scaring
Me so sweetly I start sharing
New love songs, what are you wearing
Thanks for your concern, thanks for caring

Charming

He was enchanting with his charming
Manners and his praise regarding
Her lifted her spirits dear darling
I like when you beg me to keep harming
You I am on your mind an alarming
Amount of time I'm marking
You with my teeth as you're barking
It makes her true self come out when he's charming
She swallows me like she's starving
Her legs leaking and parting
Her appetite for disgusting things keeps enlarging
Like me when she starts arching
Her ass in the air how charming

Compose

With his words he would compose
The sweetest things he would expose
His heart which I suppose
Is brave but he was her rose
She was his sunflower one of those
Bright, happy flowers they chose
To make a amazing love song they compose
Such beauty it really goes
Deep spiritually they would close
The door and teach her how to pose
He taught her how to better her shows
He gave her passion when he throws
Her against the wall he shows
Her his strength anything goes
He makes her body so hot it glows
She begged him to propose
More disgusting things she knows
He believes in her he chose
Her together beautiful things they compose

Connected

Neither of them thought they'd be so connected
They chose love, they selected
Love and together they perfected
Patience nobody feels neglected
Their connection was most unexpected
Worlds away they are always connected
She felt so loved and respected
With him with her she felt so protected
They showed each other things as they reflected
She sounds like a sow as she rested
Nobody had believed but he invested
A lot of time and energy he elected
To bring them closer, they are so connected

Consciousness

Warm uplifting words help sculpt her consciousness
I am speaking boldly to her subconsciousness
I believe in rebuilding her self-confidence
Let my words cover your walls with opulence
I elevate you, encouraging your growing prominence
My admiration for her is truly bottomless
Her deep, internal beauty always alters my consciousness
Your soul is engulfed is the warmest caress
I have always believed in your immense success
You're a huge blessing so as I bless
Us both we receive pleasure in excess
Rainbow vibes together altering our consciousness

Consistency

You no longer have to crave consistency
I'll show you a new caliber, a different pedigree
You can get your needs met consistently
I'll hold a conversation with you differently
I'm goofy and healing religiously
Stop being bored I have consistency
Lola dear Lola I'll sweep away all toxicity
With sweet songs touching you deliciously
On many levels you're the epitome
Of classic beauty, wonderful your symphony
Let me play your harp instrumentality
Warm words in a consistent gentlemanly
Manner catches her attention instantly
I'd like to make you shine brilliantly
Picture colors flowing in wild imagery
I'd like to make you taste colors, a new consistency

Consistently

You bring out the very best of me consistently
I picture you creating bliss brilliantly
She's swimming in blue waters giddily
When I speak to your soul a whole symphony
Engulfs you passionately and consistently
I encourage you often, I did it deliberately
Instead of hitting your body, I did it differently
I hit your worthiness up, sweet epiphany
I destroy all darkness in my vicinity
When I say I love you it's until infinity
I love building you up with great intensity
I'm her passionate flame, all natural electricity
I encourage, uplift, praise you religiously
She deserves true love, which I share consistently

Copy

Her beautiful tits placed on the glass make a copy
You're so petite and you've got a sexy body
You're such a babe, truly you're so foxy
Touch yourself until your panties are soggy
Then hop on the photocopier and make a copy
I know how excited it makes you to be naughty
Being a hot slut us your favorite hobby
You're touching yourself as I make it sloppy
You're such a sexbomb, you really embody
That word you slide your fingers like a jockey
She said drench me more, really shock me
They broke the mold with you so there's no other copy
I'm touching you in spots hotly so ungodly
It's making you leak through ropes super naughty
Whores copy their holes now make me a copy

Corruption

She suddenly felt his words, his corruption
She begged to be give all instruction
On her knees mouth open the suction
Of her nasty holes enjoys dirty destruction
She loved his mind was full of corruption
She filmed everything making naught production
Het pussy so wet it makes it hard to function
The nastiest bitch needs no seduction
To make her pussy have a strong eruption
You just have to show her the ultimate corruption

Cruel

I have spoken to you like a precious jewel
I've been very careful to say nice and helpful
Things if I'm not speaking in my happy usual
Way perhaps is a small taste of your cruel
Manners making people feel like a fool
Treating big fans of yours like they are miniscule
You're projecting, is the truth what's cruel
Is learning a lesson in her class of tease school
Is in session you said that I came to work to ridicule
You and I say what you did insults every molecule
Of my being instead of my fire experiencing fuel
You put it out tears falling like a pool
The opposite of love is indifference you'll
Find that if I start acting in ways unusual
Should I accept being dismissed and stay cool
Is said the truth hurts so if being truthful
To you makes you feel less than beautiful
Is because I'm reflecting you, a beast most cruel

Dare

She asked me if I would dare
To make her cum and I started to swear
Nobody has ever made me stare
At such naughtiness grabbing your long hair
My large hands around your neck decreasing your air
That's how I enjoy it, silent, now don't dare
Say being used roughly doesn't dampen your underwear
I'm slapping, biting, hitting I'm a rare
Breed I know there's nothing you care
About than cumming, I'll lay you bare
Naked and make you expose that lovely pair
Of eyes terrified like I'm a big bear
It's time for breakfast if you dare

Darkness in the Light

Sitting next to a tiger would fill anyone with fright
But not me, fear is my favorite delight
When I look at you oozing with creative insight
You're the light in the shadows, I'm darkness in the light
Let me be your favorite weakness, your kryptonite
Your beautiful mind craves most a real polite
Way of bringing out the beast in you, I might
Your big brain makes mine soar to new heights
Creative men, passionate men, know true dynamite
Is getting deep inside that kind, that really tight
Thing, making her feel quite special as I write
The sweetest love songs while you suck my mic
Open your mind fully, here comes darkness in the light.

DEGRADE

She was a filthy bitch who asked me to degrade
Her bitch is so dumb F is her grade
She loves when I'm awful, she loves being made
To do the filthiest things she displayed
Everything to me as the slut laid
Back I grabbed her firmly by her cute braid
You're fucking disgusting trash why should I degrade
A trash can she's a cumdump but she played
Like she was a queen but her body betrayed
Her longings for someone that weighed
As much as me to smother her she prayed
For her master to use her and obeyed
All his commands it was easy to persuade
Her to embrace being an object, she loves how I degrade

Destroy

She was not prepared for how I destroy
Her mind but her body starts to enjoy
Me using her holes to bring me joy
She's my cum dumpster, my Colombian sex toy
Her holes get really hot when I firmly destroy
Her with dreams of being with naughtiest boy
She rides me like I'm a horse well hung cowboy
I lasso her with rope carefully I start to employ
New techniques making her cream as I roughly destroy

Destroying

She makes the Earth shake her pussy is destroying
Everything she can't stop hotly toying
Herself I like make her lap start boiling
Is well lubricated lap I'm hotly oiling
Her engine her resolve is easy to start destroying
She says boss I feel sometimes you're employing
Me just for my body you're enjoying
This too much your panties I'm soiling
So wet you are your hungry pussy is exploiting
Its needs start singing and rejoicing
I'm dropping pleasure bombs I'm deploying
My weapon and her world is hotly destroying

Destruction

Day and night she craves intense destruction
I'm so dirty and she loves the nasty corruption
How I shove it in her mouth her mouth suction
Makes her leak as my hands and her neck make introduction
Her air lessens is absolutely delicious destruction
Her hot hole creamy begging for reproduction
She needed it nasty, she craves firm instruction
Making her lap experience shaking and eruption
I grab my camera making another dirty production
My dirty whore is my bitch with no interruption
Stretching her leaking holes with immense destruction

Disaster

She begged him to make her a disaster
Begging for more roughness and faster
She begged for him to plaster
Her face and she heard his laughter
She'll make a most beautiful disaster
Together their last made a new chapter
Pure lust was the biggest factor
In her submission it didn't matter
Whatever he asked yes please disaster
Me sir she's enchanted and he's her captor
She craves a new disgusting disaster

Distracted

He found her alone sitting there distracted
His favorite way, he quickly acted
Like a wolf, his large body flattened
Her like a pancake now she's not distracted
He took her to dark places, her body reacted
She loves how his hands contracted
Around her neck her breath subtracted
She never she would be attracted
To such disgusting things but he impacted
Her and now she'll never be distracted

Done

She asked how I do it, how is it done
I think of her, who's hotter than the sun
Then I think of how much fun
It would be to shock her and stun
Her and most importantly how to make her cum
I imagine when I write you spank your bum
I like thinking of your top coming undone
As you spread your legs whispering look what you've done
I'd like to be the reason you stick one
Finger in your mouth and taste yourself that's some
Very motivating words have I done
Well am I making it drip and start to run
Down your leg is it super sexy awesome

Dreaming

I knew it had been you I had been dreaming
About I woke up so hard, you keep heating
Me up and you beg for more beating
The harder I am, the more Michel starts creaming
I'm exploding inside her right now as she's dreaming
Making her body overheat and start steaming
She loves when I'm a deviant and demeaning
Her with her tongue the toilet she's cleaning
She thinks about me when she's streaming
Her live sex shows together we are teaming
Up and I hit her until she starts screaming
From joy and pleasure she must be dreaming

Elegant

There was exceptional focus on the most elegant
Ways to show that love becomes evident
When it touches her being, every element
Removing all stress and any impediment
Disappearing she feels the most excellent
Feelings when I speak to her in a most elegant
Tone like Song of Solomon In the old testament
Let my words and actions be most eloquent
Nothing warms her like exceptional etiquette
I'm so open, vulnerable, and warmly affectionate
I whisper you're like Coco Chanel, so elegant

Enchanted

She gasped in surprise nobody had ever enchanted
Her with such unique words he granted
Her permission to be her best and never demanded
Anything but she begged him to be commanded
He used her excitement to water the seeds he planted
When she thinks of him she is transplanted
To a new galaxy eagerly she granted
Him complete access his words landed
Deeply he was so vulnerable and candid
Her desires for pleasure he greatly expanded
She was totally bewildered, totally enchanted

Especially

When you dream, I hope it's of especially
Sweet things like being treated quite preciously
You deserve someone that addresses your complexity
With warmth and sweetness is my specialty
Being treated divinely touches every
Part of her mind, body, spirit especially
Refined treatment full of light with a feathery
Touch giving her pleasure, let me be your ecstasy
I desire to get you breathing quite heavily
Let me warmly stimulate you in every
Way possible, showing you what heavenly
Feels like she needed heat and I helpfully
Am over here singing her the sweetest melody
She loved it most being treated very respectfully
It really touched her when I share so pleasantly
She needed a refined gentleman, right now especially

Esteem

Always by you I am encouraged by the esteem
You hold my mind to the light a bright gleam
Prism colored mental pictures flow like a stream
I was thinking of the very best theme
Of love and passion is building esteem
Whispering quite softly, making you lean
Closer can I become your morphine
I like to be on your mind as you dream
Of the type of treatment that males you scream
You've got a powerful locomotive, let me be your steam
I wonder if it's possible to give you supreme
The only thing hotter than Sabrina in green
Is when she slips on one made of whipped cream
Speaking of whipped; crack, smack extreme
Loosening of all your thread, ripping every seam
I love how the more polite I am it makes you more obscene
I enjoy building you up, inhaling your growing esteem.

Exciting

She found when I entered her mind most exciting
I'm taking my time and with precision I am striking
The right chords I'm hitting her like lightning
She begged me so with rope I started tying
Her up she found my aggression so exciting
I enter her world and instantly start delighting
Her making her leak and her body starts crying
Out for more pleasure and I am mystifying
Her making her world better I'm brightening
Her body, soul, and mind she keeps trying
To stop leaking but I'm licking and biting
Her she cries out so loudly like she's dying
Nobody ever made her pussy so hot from writing
She wanted all of him, she found him most exciting

Expanding

Thinking of you makes my mind start expanding
Seeds of kindness and encouragement I'm planting
Learning your needs gives me better understanding
Nothing makes her relax like exceptional handling
I aspire to make your definition of pleasure keep expanding
I call you captivating but really your enchanting
I'll bring a picnic basket and we'll go camping
We'll wrote poetry together, our intimacy continues expanding

Express

I'm a hermit by nature but sometimes I express
Myself boldly I bloom like a torch ginger not to impress
As only to share beauty with you to excess
Sometimes instead of saying more I say less
I thought tonight of how to release your stress
All aboard the Sweet Temptations Express
I hope you enjoy things spicy and adventurous
You're more dazzling than Maui sunsets
I hope you enjoy especially sweet politeness
Let my blooming flower's fragrance obsess
I dream of your mind which makes progress
You make it safe to vulnerably never repress
Perhaps I shall make you cry happily from what I express

Favorite

Often times she would say that's my favorite
Thing about you air and I laugh a bit
She gets turned on when I make her spit
Up her food when she tries to fit
Both her hands in her mouth it might split
Her wide open but I don't give shit
She loves being a disgusting dog I make her admit
Everything she gives me everything and will permit
Me anything I like marking her as I bit
Her big ass she starts leaking down her slit
The effect on her body is impossible to counterfeit
He makes her a filthy mess and then get
To cleaning your puddle dog and then sit
Wait I show you another new thing to be your favorite

Favorite Flower

She told me roses are her favorite flower
Which I didn't know but our
Beauty expands as we reflect our power
Our strength in unity how we empower
Pushing through the sidewalk a wildflower
When she blooms it allows her outer
Beauty to reveal a dazzling rose shower
You have great inner beauty I'll say it louder
Your essence oozes, you're my favorite flower

Filthy Slave

She volunteered to be my filthy slave
She loved the depth of my mind, how depraved
I am and she said I'll do anything I'll behave
Like the filthiest fucking whore you will save
Your juices for me slut, drippings of my filthy slave
She trustee master and became most brave
Grabbing her by her hair dragging to a cave
I'll fuck you so senseless you'll feel like your in your grave
Giving you pleasure and pain in one huge wave
My dick brings her ecstasy, and she loves to rave
About how she loves being my filthy fucking slave
You're dripping everywhere I make you misbehave
Another orgasm master like the one you just gave

Fire

She's as hot as lava is like playing with fire
She makes me see red and experience burning desire
Her body banging like gunfire
I like to warm her and make her perspire
I should like her to catch on fire
In her heart with urges to go higher
To see the world differently, even brighter
She asks if I'll put on the handcuffs tighter
She leaking fuel everywhere and I'm her lighter
Drip, drip, drip she's leaking through her attire
She puts me totally in her mouth fitting the entire
Thing as she spits and drools sexual multiplier
She's so hot her nickname is fire

First

When him there be many first
Time experiences he was well versed
In perversions he was the absolute worst
Pervert and in gave her incredible thirst
She said thank you for so many first
Times with me he is her sunburst
She was a disgusting bitch he cursed
Slapping her until her body burst
With pleasure she hotly nursed
Him sucking eagerly headfirst
If she wants a kiss she swallows first

Fit

My professor is super fit
Is admire her body very much I admit
That I enjoy all her fashion, every outfit
She's so smart, has such great wit
She is so sensual she's always starts emit
Motivation for me to become as fit
As she's firm and far from delicate
She's the cherry on top the banana split
My professor is on fire, she's so lit
Her mind has such a wonderful benefit
On my mind how she motivates me to be fit

Flesh

She desires to taste my flesh
Thinking of me as she rests
Slowly nibbling and biting her breast
In her dreams I slowly caress
Her exciting her in new levels her flesh
Crave me to roughly use and test
Her slowly I am bringing out her best
My tongue licking her slowly as I refresh
I'll do anything to make her success
She wears little and even less
She's revealing her succulent flesh

Forgotten

She said she didn't like being forgotten
I laughed you're being spoiled rotten
So many things I've gotten
You so you'll never feel forgotten
I'm a flower come lay in my pollen
I treat her special, for from common
I treat her very special, support uncommon
He would never leave her, she's never forgotten

Four

It's inspiring you made one butterfly shine four
Times, what a fascinating way you store
Your treasures such placement makes me feel more
Appreciated and thank you for your
Swift response I do hope to expand more
Glowing is always when I dream of one I adore
I am reminded why occasionally I wake at four
In the morning always such a pleasure
It's like double rainbows start to pour
Out and I am reminded of your immense allure
You make my inner lion really roar
By glowing, blossoming butterfly times four

Gardening

I have learned from practice excellent gardening
The biggest thing is patience my darling
Darling if I called you beyond sparkling
Would you see in my eyes a wild stargazing
Lily I'm an exotic flower and I enjoy gardening
Let me be the lightning when skies are darkening
My touch electric with perfect targeting
 Your body has the most beautiful marbling
I hope when I say such things it is starting
To make you warm, is this true heartening
I clean the dirtiest gardens, I love gardening

Gentle

Nothing felt better than bathing her in gentle
Sweet words she needed kindness it was fundamental
Massaging her scalp and brain letting all mental
Stress release together we are being experimental
An experiment in feeling touched most gentle
She makes me be a gentleman the most monumental
Way to bring her pleasure is worship at temple
She makes me sing gleefully like from a hymnal
Let me wash you in a beautiful baptismal
Pool of healing I'd like to make your lips tremble
Licking her lips makes it better, especially when I'm gentle

Handcuffed

The only way to get her focused is handcuffed
When it comes to handcuffs she can't get enough
Ye please she prefers it rough
Being social for her is too tough
Thankfully she likes other fun stuff
Especially if it involves being handcuffed
The turkey isn't the only thing getting stuffed
She was anti-social but she discussed
Things that made her bust
Out laughing she will erupt
Only if you get her handcuffed

In Heat

I made her so warm she's now in heat
Flexibility is key she practices her feet
In her mouth nothing will defeat
Her she longs for the day we meet
How roughly I'll use my piece of meat
Just thinking of it gets her in heat
She will bounce, she will leap
She will experience mistreatment so sweet
Using her body like an athlete
Covered in spit walking down the street
Men looking at her like they'd like eat
Her she begs me master please mistreat
Me more it makes her overheat
Now she's an even bigger bitch in heat

Intense

He made her feel very intense
Things meeting him made sense
He kept her in epic suspense
His love left her no need for defense
She opened to feelings most intense
He gave her luxury, he spared no expense
The desires he created such suspense
He created desire in her most immense
His heart full of sweet essence
It made her feel things most intense

Invest

She felt honored he chose to invest
In her she felt truly blessed
He spent time helping her be her best
He focused on her mind more than her chest
He gave her confidence, she impressed
Him and showed how wise he was to invest
Vulnerably he boldly expressed
Himself and the way that he expressed
Himself made her body possessed
She touches herself often he doesn't protest
She knew all her needs are addressed
Her biggest believer, he suggests
Her be nastier and she progressed
Now she calls him totally undressed
What an interesting opening to invest

Jizz Junkie

I know a really, really filthy jizz junkie
She's swallow more bananas than a monkey
If she doesn't get jizz often she gets grumpy
So I fill her hot holes with jazz, she's so spunky
Swallowing so many random dicks, she's a jazz junkie
She begs me please daddy punish me
Putting her hot leaking ass over my knee
She does it for attention and also for money
Sticking it in her ass makes her pussy so runny
Dick for breakfast, lunch, dinner she's so hungry
For it she's the biggest, nastiest jizz junkie

Kindling

He returned to her noticing her fire was dwindling
He started fanning her flames quickly rekindling
Her passionately, he said it's time to start shifting
He lifted her spirits, she needed uplifting
Words use all the negativity for kindling
Let it burn, let go of all that was existing
And rise from the ashes phoenix, I'm assisting
Her in gathering and collecting all the kindling
She forgave everything, the fire is whisking
Away the past and now the present is gifting
Her new opportunities start risking
Everything again your spirit is glistening
Beautiful orchid my words keep misting
Use it to propel you, use the kindling

King

She treats me and calls me her King
I hit her so hard she enjoys the sting
I take her to new places I bring
Her up and place her in a sex swing
Like a little doll I wildly fling
Her she loves being nasty for her King
In the shower she will dance and sing
Begging him to use her as his plaything
My hands around her neck hotly ring
Her pleasure button I grab some string
To tie her up apple in mouth pig served to her king

Kiss Here

Her new tattoo said kiss here
So I told her to bring the camera near
So I could better look and even leer
You're body fills mine with cheer
I want to see you cheerlead as I kiss here
Let me kiss you slowly and softly dear
Let me make you smile and have a happy tear
Pull that bodysuit to the side, show your rear
Even more so I can start to kiss here

Late

The silly student had lost track of time, was late
He reminded her of how he would dilate
Her eyes he knew how to really fascinate
Her he thought her a lesson about making him wait
He would smother her using all of his weight
It may be your very last time being late
Is more important earn money than masturbate
Is first things first she must never hesitate
Is making money more important than fellate
Her friend the bitch can always ejaculate
On your face later on not on a date
You're serving your hot ass up on a plate
I will shackle the bitch like an inmate
Do not make be scold or berate
You bitch is first rule is never be late

Learning

She asked how I learned, I started learning
How to write poems from my grandma in turning
Our obstacles into triumph we start earning
Our mental muscles and I'm constantly learning
For instance, you expand my meaning of yearning
My words melt all problems I'm churning
Out authentic vulnerability what starts returning
Is practice in being quite discerning
I'm more interested in can I make start burning
In the most pleasant ways cool heartburning
By listening to your desires, I start learning

Leaving

She begged me, she was pleading
Please don't leave I'm never leaving
Princess it was I that was perceiving
Ways to get you everything you're dreaming
About making your lap start creaming
I'm licking your ass, it's steaming
You beg for more mistreatment, more demeaning
Things I love most when she's weeping
Tears everywhere makeup ruined achieving
A new level of nasty she's heaving
Begging me to piss on her, start relieving
Me I make her start hotly leaking
She is showing me things she is sneaking
Flashing my in public such peeking
Excites me, mi amor I'm never leaving

Liberate

Nobody before was able to help liberate
Her but I make her pupils start to dilate
Our paths crossed, must have been fate
I whisper the most interesting things to fascinate
You I'm taking great liberties to liberate
You in new ways that deeply stimulate
The best of you, entering your pearly gate
You reply look at the beauty you create
You are absolutely my favorite playmate
Centerfold I'm folding your center as your hips gyrate
I like being a reason you start to masturbate
Lay back and let me continue to titillate
You even more as I continue to liberate

Liberating

I am liberal but also very liberating
When I speak her heart starts vibrating
He had touched her soul by stating
The truth she was learning pulsating
I will push and bend you in very liberating
Positions your juices collected I'm hydrating
Myself with your tears I start activating
Inside her and now things start calculating
Her favorite thing about him was his dominating
Nature the inner slut inside her he's creating
The biggest, most disgusting bitch I'm detonating
A bomb in her ass she's so nauseating
She's retching and reaching new lows degrading
Her just helped her with more liberating

Liberation

She was shocked alive, he woke up her damnation
Her shackles released, total liberation
He set the wild wolf out to hunt his deviant creation
Would become the biggest bitch in the nation
When he speaks she feels such joy and elation
He helped her find hunger in a different location
He led her to her self-created salvation
I didn't save you bitch true liberation
Comes from eating ravenously I'm her temptation
The hungry wolf tied experiencing pink vibrations
Angelica licks Michel with much adoration
Dirty disgusting pig slut gets heated from degradation
Nothing warms her holes like extreme humiliation
He took liberties with her ass, his expert liberation

Little Volcano

She sent me a picture of a little volcano
But not hers I like when she bravely shows
Me her lava as it expands and starts to glow
Sit on top of my face and let your stress flow
Everywhere my explosive little volcano
The pressure inside her continues to grow
I'm making it steamy like lava meeting snow
Sweetness and naughty is her favorite combo
She begs me to watch her use her dildo
Her big pussy lips eating her little micro
Bikini I'm reaching her pleasure plateau
Tasting her juices is like tasting a rainbow
I've got her so hot she's ready to blow
I make her explosive, my hot little volcano

Loves More

Together they would argue who loves more
She said you bring out the most impure
Things making her put four
Fingers in her mouth until it is sore
She loves being dirty, she loves more
Disgusting things licking the bathroom floor
Ripping her soul he tore
A new opening hard to ignore
What's she's becoming most impure
She was mouse that made the lion roar
I love her the most, but she loves more

Maid

She asked me to be my naughty maid
She bent over her ass she displayed
Such gratitude she said you made
Me feel so special her hands strayed
Under a skirt she's such a naughty maid
Bitch you will make sure to braid
Your hair her eyes conveyed
Such desires and love I invade
Her thoughts of the pervert portrayed
She begged me slap her and degrade
Her she'll do anything to persuade
Me to let her serve as my filthy maid

Merry

It is Christmas today but I'm merry
Because I met you, you're so very
Beautiful and I imagine feeding you a cherry
My hands gliding over you barely
Touching you like a glittering fairy
I hope I make you smile and merry
Into the bath I slowly carry
You bathing you in light it's scary
To be so in love but it makes me most merry

Mi Amor

Butterflies riot when I whisper mi amor
I give her quality things from the store
She sticks in her mouth four
Fingers today I am helping her explore
The different levels of mi amor
She begged me to mistreat her more
She said like a dog treat me poor
So I make her lick the bathroom floor
I make her feel sexy and glamor
She loves my energy and I make her soar
Her juices start leaking out and I pour
Her spit all over the face of mi amor

Mind

She likes it when she's on my mind
I opened her eyes when she was blind
Now pleasures continue being refined
She loves how I'm a pervert yet kind
There she was waiting for me to find
Her she whispered would you mind
Grabbing my braids, take me from behind
My depravity made her clothes slimed
Everyone say how I like to unwind
Covered in spit as he assigned
Her to be a bigger bitch she's primed
For more disgusting destruction it's been on my mind

Missing

His little dirty dog went missing
She came back begging for forgiving
If that's what you want what you're wishing
For open your mouth as I'm pissing
You're my toilet and gladly assisting
Me filthy fucking bitch is listening
Very close her body is glistening
She happy agrees, no resisting
Make me the dirtiest bitch she kept insisting
She likes drink my piss I'm gifting
Her be my toilet now she's living
To be a pisswhore I'm sniffing
Her and slowly start quizzing
On her face is a hot load I'm jizzing
All over her clothes and not missing
Anything on the floor start licking

Nasty

Privately with me she is most nasty
She begs me mistreat her more daddy
She loves submitting, does it gladly
She's enchanted and falling madly
In love with the one who makes her nasty
My hands around her throat fatly
Being choked makes her cry gladly
She loves my orders, especially the nasty

Nerdy

You inspire me to start speaking nerdy
You make all sorts of thoughts happen so wordy
You make me embrace my most quirky
Parts I like making your ears perky
Can I capture your attention by speaking extra nerdy
Drink my sweet nectar hummingbird, come birdie
Is much sweetness here are you very thirsty
My message loud and clear you are worthy
I'm not kitten when I say your quite purrrrrdy
Seeing you makes my legs less sturdy
You bring out my playfulness, my most nerdy

Nobility

She said most all of she loves my nobility
I can see the desires in her eyes visually
I make her heart experience a symphony
Of cherished, I touch her differently
She may soon find my nobility
When she's handcuffed with no ability
To move the happiest in captivity
She loves how I see her brilliantly
How I slap her ass most friskily
Thinking of me gets her most explicitly
Turned on with exceptional chivalry
She will follow me to the epitome
Of pleasure she surrenders willingly
She is turned on by such amazing nobility

Noble

You bring out the very most noble
Parts of me as you whisper be bolder
My large hands massage your shoulder
You love my support, I'm so vocal
About you winning you're my total
Motivation for becoming more noble
You glisten and shine like an opal
Constantly making your mouth an oval
You're most beautiful in global
Beauty contests you make all immobile
Your stunning self constantly brings out the noble

Nurturing

She knew nothing before of what nurturing
Was before him but his consistent worshipping
Encouraging her always and furthering
Her life, her goals, she loves nurturing
He came into her life like a tidal wave surging
She's riding my wave of light, she's surfing
You can do it, I'm encouraging
Her more today than ever before by serving
I came into her life to give endless nurturing

Obsessed

She couldn't help herself, he made he obsessed
She recorded herself often undressed
She loved hearing his encouragement he expressed
Himself like no other, she was often perplexed
At his creative mind it made her obsessed
Thinking of what he would do or say next
Maybe he'll slap the shit out of her chest
Perhaps he'll clamp her luscious breasts
Maybe he'll handcuff her, she's under arrest
He knew how to bring out her very best
She was enamored by how much he blessed
Her with love and lust she's becoming more obsessed

Overflowing

When I think of you kindness starts overflowing
Though usually reserved you make me outgoing
Encouragements and sweet words keep flowing
As I think you enjoy where this is going
Love is in actions and I'm bravely showing
Her new definitions of mind blowing
Pleasure carefully my words start slowing
Down thinking of you as you start glowing
Kindness makes her heart start overflowing

Overwhelming

She's in a micro bikini her large lips overwhelming
Me her pussy covered by just a string
I'm taking her to new dimensions let me bring
You energy so overwhelming you can't help but sing
The raw eroticism to her pussy is overwhelming
She's leaking everywhere, completely melting
I'm pulling her hair firmly, slapping her hamstring
I've got a mask on because I'm going snorkeling
In her ocean I'm giving her my everything
I'm in her heaven and I'm wholly worshipping
Making her mind bloom like flowers in the spring
She's turned on in multiple dimensions, so overwhelming

Picnic

She suggested I take my grandma on a picnic
Grandma asked me whose the most beautiful chick
You know, I replied sexy bitch and she said quick
Write something that makes her heart have an uptick
Dear won't you show me your pretty lipstick
Making you smile as I take you to pick
Fresh exotic flowers as we start to click
Santa I can explain, dear Saint Nick
I tried behaving but she creates a magic trick
She makes inspiration explode she's a matchstick
Her Louboutins dancing on top of powder keg she kicks
My mind into oblivion I just want to lick
Her mind and feed her fresh fruit on a picnic

Pink Hints

In the sunrise there were a lot of pink hints
Pinks my favorite color, I liked it even since
I met you, you're like a sunrise hence
Forth you shall be known as pink hints
Your energy makes my heart lightly wince
In a most wonderful, purely pink sense
I held you inhaling beautiful pink scents
Smelling your pink makes me quite tense
Politeness combined with pretty pink hints
As your garden experiences a pink mist
She didn't know such beautiful pink could exist
How does if get hotter than your pink lips
Perhaps she like imagine there's a prince
In her garden tending to her pink bits
Your pink is my favorite fragrance
Everything about her oozes pink decadence
I've found streams of pleasure mouthing pink hints

Piss

She thinks of him when she starts to piss
He was able to make her dismiss
All thoughts of being a queen she couldn't resist
She begged him, she would insist
Please sir let me drink your piss
All she knew was that this
Man drove her wild he gets
Her so heated on her face he spits
Being used disgustingly give her bliss
Now open your mouth for more piss

Potential

One of the most potent actions is increasing potential
I believe in you since our initial
Meeting she loves kindness, it's critical
That I remind her of the most essential
Things which is she has infinite potential
Let me lift you up, be positively influential
I drew her using many of my colored pencils
My mind is sharp, let me be instrumental
In helping you with every utensil
I have make sure to take notes with your pencil
The warmest, most loving, and simple
Message embrace your femininity, your sensual
Desires and dreams the dirtiest and most simple
I help her find pleasures wildly, exponential
Levels I love helping increase your potential

Power

She said that my poem gave her power
It actually reminded her that every hour
That passes without sad, bitter, sour
Feelings is harnessing her tremendous brainpower
She can overcome anything with her willpower
I was happy to warmly remind her of the power
She already has and encourage her bloom wildflower
Swallow the negativity powerfully devour
It all harness and enjoy your sunflowers
That you planted I mean if cauliflower
Can become pizza than you have tremendous power

Practicing

He made his dog be constantly practicing
She loved to be of use without even asking
He grabbed her neck so hard he's grasping
Her so firmly her eyes water and she's gasping
For air she was his toy to use for practicing
His huge body began regularly smashing
Her nipples clamps, he was roughly clasping
Making her ass so red it's maddening
She reads these things and her hands are traveling
To her clit she's in awe of his perversions is baffling
She loved being of service in his practicing

Prescribing

She's sickie wickie so I am prescribing
Unique medicine, sweet healing writing
Bathing her in healing blue light I'm applying
My mind to get her sickness to start subsiding
Something to make her feel better I'm prescribing
Incredible healing colorful and high vibing
Massaging her temples with electrifying
Pulses lay back receive healing I'm inviting
Your sickness to leave taking a towel and drying
You off again I'm bathing in blue light trying
To make your sickness leave I'm guiding
You to wonder if this is slowly delighting
You when I whisper, you're so striking
Making your sickness leave as fast as lightning
In the darkness her starts shining
Healing vibrations mixed with the most exciting
Words doctors orders I'm carefully inciting
You to think of what makes you start biting
Your lip, there's a medicine worth prescribing

Professor

He started whispering imagine that your professor
She is bending over wearing a leather
Dress her ass exposed she's starting her lecture
All you can do is drool at her hot treasure
She thinks of being told to pleasure
Her, stick your tongue deep in your professor
I'm slowly making her the hottest bitch ever
Nobody before had ever made it so hot she never
Imagined it was possible to get any wetter
But I know just how to apply pressure
On her clit I mercilessly teasing her forever
She begged for release crying out I'll do whatever
You want, I give her horniness beyond measure
I will help her to seduce her teacher, her sexy professor

Protected

With him she was always protected
She was his medicine and injected
Him with dirty desires he expected
Her success so he invested
A lot into making her feel protected
His energy and gifts she accepted
Thinking of his blue eyes as she rested
No part of her shall ever be neglected
She felt believed in, they perfected
Hotness together they melted
All obstacles, she was always respected
They are so close, very connected
He was her warmth, he always protected

Prowess

I've been complimented on my mental prowess
You inspire me to have more finesse
Finding words that ease and lessen stress
I like when you feel uplifted yes
You are an inspiration, you increase my prowess
Finding even deeper vulnerability to express
You've been so helpful, you quicken my process
When you share that you're warm my success
Come sit by this fire, there's quite an excess
Amount of fuel you're leaking, can I address
Any unmet needs or desires, I deliver like Federal Express
Great questions are derived with excellent prowess

Queen

She really wanted badly to be a Queen
So I whispered in her ear why don't you lean
Back and receive me slowly licking you clean
She likes reading the hottest most obscene
Things to her and I'm over her making both scream
Fuck yes this is how you treat a Queen
Slowly I stick my fingers in between
Her warming hole I'm very keen
To lick every inch of your body and mind I mean
Let me give you a huge surge of dopamine
I'll perk your body up more than caffeine
And make you redefine what it is to be a Queen

Real Cat

She asked me if that was a real cat
It made me howl because she's a hellcat
She's a hell of a woman matter of fact
Her hair is hella beautiful it makes me react
 She ran her hands in her hair it's a real cat
She calls me a nut, but she's an acrobat
She makes hearts fly in the air total circus act
She hits me with her hands I'd like to chat
About her hitting me she's so striking it's just that
She's not afraid to hit me like it's Mortal Kombat
She brings out the sweetest in me I pat
Her on her head, yes, she's a real cat

Reassured

She needed to hear it, so he reassured
Her I'll never abandon you baby, she heard
His deep voice as his blue eyes stirred
Her emotions driving her to new levels of absurd
Never before had a man been so good with words
He spoke lovingly to her, he reassured
Her that she was desired and treasured
She loved it naughty but she preferred
When he was super sweet, he transferred
His warmth to her he was nectar to his hummingbird
I love you always and forever, she felt reassured

Reconnect

When I think of you things start to reconnect
Know you've been through the ringer you wept
Oceans of tears and you experienced much neglect
I whispered I've always carefully kept
You in my prayers I imagined you slept
Very little allow me to help you recollect
Relaxation and pleasure such loving dialect
I can't help checking on you I checked
And it's been too long since you received correct
Warmth I'm a flower and my favorite insect
Little honey bee roll around and inspect
The lovely pollen covered in love I'll protect
Your heart neither perfect but we beautifully reflect
The power of healing the more we reconnect

Red

She's is the victim of my desires so she's seeing red
I bit her very often, she totally soaked her bedspread
She thought it was her end, this would be her deathbed
I've awaken the horniest devil in her instead
You're looking in the mirror at all the red
Knowing filth and depravity lie ahead
You think of me every time you shed
A tear from your leaking lap my belt left a tread
Against your body using your juices on my bread
Filthy kitten so hungry for my milk, I keep her well fed
Her pussy is as slick as ice and I'm her bobsled
Sliding, slipping, moving fast inside your head
Wearing your smallest bikini just a thread
Of fabric as I lick her lips I lipread
Her a story that really watered her flowerbed
I'm spreading her open, the pleasure is widespread
Think of me when you're touching yourself in your bed
I'll make everything you see and feel red

Red Bottom

She said she'd sell her soul for a pair of red bottom
Heels made by Christian Louboutin I said um
Babe, I've got you baby and I've got some
Interesting ways get on your knees come
Lick your ass juices off of my thumb
Spanking her until she cries from her red bottom
I'm beating her ass like a war drum
She needs a man with a very large income
She's a mermaid and swallows all the seaman
She's blindfolded, gagged, chained it's awesome
When she thinks of me a river starts to run
Down her leg at her she dresses like a nun
I'm her personal Christ my crucifix is in her bum
Come lick your ass juices off my dick it tastes awesome
The type of girl that would swallow all my cum
Deserves being used roughly stick out your tongue
It's dinner time dear your top is undone
Suck my soul, I'll get you your red bottoms
Be my filthy slave bitch, it'll be a lot of fun

Refreshing

I had forgotten how lovely and refreshing
Her energy is even though lately had been depressing
I reminded her to be certain and stop guessing
Her heartache and sadness needed addressing
So I sang to her a reminder I'm professing
From day one you've always been impressing
Me and that tension I'm carefully pressing
Just take deep breaths and keep progressing
She always can reach me when it gets distressing
You're such a wonderful and tremendous blessing
Softly, warmly, gently her heart I'm caressing
Healing light and words provided needed refreshing

Replaceable

She said that all her cows had come to stable
Just pieces of meat to her, easily replaceable
She is totally and wonderfully insatiable
Making up this interesting fairy tale fable
But reaching her heart is totally unattainable
To her, I am not special, easily replaceable
I hope one day she focuses on her vocational
Skills I find her singing captivating, inescapable
I learned a lot from her, it's been educational
I'll always remember her singing as sensational
I find her singing so soothing and inspirational
I had forgotten that my heart was breakable
Until she showed me that I was easily replaceable

Respect

My grandma taught me everything I know about respect
She said if you're ever on the front page I expect
For it to be something honorable I select
My words carefully because you deserve respect
The world needs more sweetness and intellect
When I call you stunning, I simply reflect
Your radiance knowing nobody is perfect
I make it clear that it's safe all I will always protect
Your heart, your mind is my favorite subject
I'd like to be on it my words slowly swept
Away all negativity she couldn't believe it kept
Getting even better she laid back and started to accept
Politeness, sincerity, vulnerability, I stepped
Forth bravely showing her a new level of respect

Scolding

She begged me to not give her a scolding
She saw the fire in my eyes start smoldering
She thought of running, she thought of bolting
She then she was reminded of his withholding
She would do anything for his handholding
She knew she had not done her best and deserved scolding
His hand refused to move, she felt like molting
She would never again do something so revolting
He would give her a most serious jolting
He would make her melt, he's molding
He lifts her up like nobody, he's upholding
Her and she'll do anything for his slaveholding
Apologize like you mean it bitch, do you need more scolding?

Sculpting

It had been a long time since she's been sculpting
When she felt angry of like sulking
She ate those energies for bulking
Up her new batch of wonders she's sculpting
Again and through all ties she's cutting
She severs it all, taking time, adjusting
She was a winner always to me there's nothing
Quite like her colorful, dazzling, unique sculpting
I have enjoyed it so much, you're really something
Her expert hands are warmly and smoothly cupping
Her clay as the talent starts busting
Out everywhere she remembered totally trusting
She finds herself once again sculpting

Shower

She wakes up and starts recording her shower
Thinking of her wolf that will devour
Her she loves knowing he will overpower
Her and make her do things sweet and sour
She can't stop rubbing herself every hour
She loves his perversity, his big power
He makes her bark and beg louder
She's happy being his bitch, couldn't be prouder
She always spreads her ass wide in the shower

SINNER

I told her openly and honestly I'm a sinner
You make me want to reach deep within my inner
Soul, you make me feel like a winner
I love your curves and never wish you thinner
You make me pray a lot; I don't want to be a sinner
I imagine the last supper, a most interesting dinner
Feelings drown me but you motivate be to be an Olympic swimmer
I'm an open book, studying the scripture
I'm an open vessel, a total blank slate, a beginner
I've never seen a woman shine like you, you shimmer
You bring out the best of me leaving behind being a sinner

Sore

Her neck, butt, shoulders, and back were sore
Like a cat she slept on the floor
She said I remember that you're
Very good at helping me restore
My body to relief when she's sore
I spoke to her if her feminine allure
When I grabbed her glutes she swore
She gasped at how playfully I'd explore
Making her body bask in the splendor
My strong hands made her start to roar
She needed firm touching and more
When she's satisfied she asks for an encore
She enjoys firmness and I'm hardcore
With something very sweet at the core
Now she's feeling even tighter than before
She loved how her spirits would soar
When he helped her become less sore

Stir

It happened slowly, he expertly began to stir
Up her inner beast she begged please sir
Please help me redefine guilty pleasure
Many men had tried awaking the bitch in her
But his was the nicest and naughtiest mixture
She was still amazed how his words stir
Up her juices he stayed, I know you prefer
To be a disgusting, filthy, nasty bitch his whisper
Made her start leaking and a low whimper
She was a bitch in heat nobody made it wetter
He made her body, spirit, and mind purr
Like a happy cat he wrote the most impure
Things and he attached her tight collar
He made her ass purple his brutal transfer
Of energy made her inner whore stir

Stray

There's a certain type of woman I'd never stray
From, there is a particular way
That I express myself I hope I may
Reach your heart hopefully I can convey
That she deserves a man that doesn't stray
You're very refined and beautiful in a classic way
Such lovely hands and nails you display
Exceptionally well I hope you have a lovely day
Dear you are my definition of gourmet
It's probably been too long since you received a bouquet
Of flowers you're a petite sophisticate, a filet
Mignon and you are sizzling like the sun's ray
A woman of her caliber deserves to not have anyone stray

Submit

She longed for a man that she would have to submit
To seeing is believing now she must admit
How hot being my filthy slave makes her get
So horny she's thinking how hard I bit
Her ass and how she'll never be able to forget
How amazing she feels when she has to submit
I like slapping her ass and rubbing her clit
I make her start dripping down her tight slit
She begs me to use her holes for my benefit
She's drooling over my cock, there's a large pile of spit
She's leaving wet spits everyplace that she sits
She said I love being your slave and openly admit
It makes her feel so happy to eagerly submit

Sunset

She sent me a picture, she's a sunset
It reminded me of the first time that we met
Something that extraordinary I'll never forget
I think meeting you by flying on a jet
I certainly have known it could get
So extraordinary, I haven't told you yet
You've made me lose track of the alphabet
I can't think of what your best asset
Is but I do know it feels like a racing corvette
Your blond streaked hair is an excellent pallet
Meeting you was like hitting 00 in roulette
What's really artwork is your silhouette
You are far more beautiful than any sunset

Supermam

I'm never mistaken for Superman, I'm Supermam
Excuse me miss wow you're so glam
I think I found where the stairway to heaven began
You hit me like a bomb hits Japan
You're truly super, you're Supermam
You melt me quicker than a snowman
In the desert so thirsty in need of a fan
Standing next to you getting a suntan
Let me increase the pearl inside your clam
I'm melting like butter all over your ham
If you enjoy your hair pulled by a caveman
I'll feed you candy and we'll go in my van
I've got a really quick trigger, wait attention span
I'm easily distracted no shots fired by a minuteman
I was just predicting your future a rainbow weatherman
I predict you'll keep raining over and over again
Does that sound super, does it sound Supermam?

Sweetie

She likes to call me sweet, I'm her sweetie
She loves being treated richly not cheaply
The kind of men that give to the needy
Are her favorite he looks quite full of seedy
Intentions but his mouth spoke so sleekly
She begged for sweeter, she begged meekly
Let me slowly blow you away completely
I'll do it very dirty then clean neatly
There's a real use for a quiet man that discreetly
Whispers things like you really turn me on sweetie

Sweetly Divine

She called me divinely sweet, I think sweetly divine
Is an accurate description of this friend of mine
I'd like to use marble to sculpt her incredibly fine
Body as it ages so excellently like wine
Sabrina is the type of art I call fine
She inspires the most incredible and sweetly divine
Send me off with wild love indeed you'll find
That when it comes to wild you redefine
What happens when beauty and intelligence combine
To form what I would describe as sublime
The only thing better than her amazing behind
Is her wildness, she's totally one of a kind
She's wildly intelligent, such a sexy mind
They broke the mold when they made you, that's genuine
You bring out the best in me, the sweetly divine

Teaming

The two of us are a team we are teaming
Up to make fortunes and make screaming
She shows off her tits lusciously leaning
Over as I increase her temperature she's steaming
She begs me for a really fierce beating
She gets what she wants we are teaming
Is make her a whore while she's streaming
On her cam making her pussy start creaming
She loves my mistreatment the more demeaning
The better in her French maid outfit cleaning
Being the biggest pervert, giving a new meaning
To disgusting we do it dirty as we're teaming

Thought

When it comes to pleasure I put a lot of thought
Into what will get you absolutely hot
When you're heated and I see a drop
Falling down your leg it really got
Me motivated it's time someone taught
You what discipline means you thought
You were composed but my words effect you a lot
My little doll tries her best to squat
On me and her body and mind fought
With everything it had but the thought
Of me spanking you made you get caught
Misbehaving touching yourself as I tie a knot
Bound, and gagged, submission can't be bought
You desire to be the nastiest, you desire to be taught
Now being pointed is your only thought

Toilet

He ordered her to start licking the toilet
She's being so disgusting his pet
Dog obeys eagerly now get
Your mouth open, you're my toilet
She's so hot that he's going to let
Her drink his piss the jet
Sprays down her throat and I bet
Reading this gets her super wet
I make the bitch leak and sweat
Using her tongue every letter in the alphabet
In my ass as I use her as my toilet

Too Sweet

How lovely to hear I'm too sweet
I tried looking away but you defeat
All my efforts you glow with heat
Sensational hair, hot eyes, what a treat
You are dear, l I'd like to meet
You and get to know you next week
You run through my mind like and athlete
You're very refined, quite elite
I'll be happy to stay upbeat
Thinking of you makes me way too sweet

Training

She asked me for specific training
Teach me to be a bitch she's obtaining
New levels of disgusting and no complaining
She cries out loudly, howling exclaiming
He was glad to assist in her training
She pushed deeper in her mouth she's gaining
More attention and I'm staining
Her shirt with saliva and making
Her walk around town how fascinating
He showed her a lifestyle she's maintaining
Herself quite well, she's great at training

Tranquility

Hearing from her I experience tranquility
She fills me with high quality energy
Makes me feel capable of overcoming any disability
She makes it safe for ultimate vulnerability
She's medicine, she's tranquility
Makes it comfortable to express any sensitivity
Hearing from her gives me much virility
There's something unique about her ability
To bring out my best, her availability
Is thin but wow her fertility
Thank you for helping me experience tranquility

Tree

She wished for her teacher under the tree
She longed to be used so sweetly
She asked me to cover her mouth in pee
Between us we find an opportunity
If it's Christmas why aren't you under my tree
Making you behave so pleasantly
Increasing your definition of heavenly
Gifts for her came in plenty
She felt so special, so full of glee
For Christmas she begged me
To mistreat her so miserably
In her mouth fingers are three
Now four she's deepthroating I see
Her naked presenting herself under my tree

Trimming

I am in my boss' hedges doing much trimming
I can't believe she just came out of her living
Room naked, she came outside warmly grinning
I told her wait, start from the beginning
She said I was sitting on her imprinting
Her with a stamp this has nice fitting
Leaving her speechless makes hot sinning
She was rubbing her kindling her hips spinning
She ordered me to pick her up and start pinning
Her against the door like wrestling I'm winning
She loved a man that took her to extra innings
Now I'm on her pond like a rock skipping
She invited me in her pool now we're swimming
By pool I mean bathtub, it's brimming
I wonder if she enjoys a long lasting rimming
My tongue is strong and has been called prize-winning
I see a burning bush, I've ignited her kindling
I hit her brain with well versed trimming

Trusting

She had finally found a man worthy of trusting
He encouraged her unlike most men wasn't rushing
His slow and deliberate pace had her humming
She couldn't recognize herself, what she's becoming
Is a filthy fucking bitch she was trusting
Her master his attention made her panties need adjusting
He got her extremely heated, he's so fucking
Hot in her mouth all her fingers she's stuffing
The saliva makes a huge mess its running
All down her face and lap she's cussing
At him she's desperate for filthy, dirty loving
She imagines his tongue each time he's buzzing
Her clit is engorged he's making her start huffing
No man ever made her nipples start puffing
Out sometimes she just starts shoving
Her fingers inside dreaming of a master worth trusting

Two Men

She drank some alcohol and then went with two men
She stuck her foxtail plug deep within
Her ass and then started letting them pin
Her and slap her face it really made her grin
She loves being made to do things especially when
She's taken like a slut by two men
One shoved his cock roughly deep in
Her mouth and being a fuckdoll made her grin
She loved when they slapped her hotly on her skin
She wants all the cum she's a sperm bin
A filthy cumbucket now she begs two men
To come all over her mouth and chin
She dreams about doing it over and over again

Understanding

He showed her a new level of understanding
She lived his orders, he wasn't demanding
She gladly gave her leash handing
It to her master he was outstanding
He reached deep within her understanding
His hands on her body made a swift landing
Inside her mind he's carefully planting
Seeds of naughty she starts panting
Like a bitch in heat he's enchanting
Her giving her obsessions true understanding

Very New

The feelings she felt were overwhelming and very new
She could tell he was rare, very few
Men excited her and as her body flew
Through the air her master just threw
Her around like a doll she's really into
Being treated like a bitch, it's very new
He pushed her mouth open busting through
Her limits he made her lick his shoe
He beat her body black and blue
He was an expert master and he knew
Just how to make her lap as sticky as glue
She begged him to call his whole crew
Lining up stranger after stranger she blew
They called her the nastiest bitch, very true
She embraced her inner whore, it was very new

Vibrating

In your presence my soul starts vibrating
You arrest my attention, there's no escaping
The vibe you put out is rainbow charged, fascinating
Your internal continues growing, never fading
I enjoy your intellect; it makes mine start vibrating
At a higher frequency I feel my creativity waking
You should know how inspiring you are making
Me a better version of myself so I'm stating
Vulnerable things bravely, you are aiding
Me in growth you're energy is invigorating
I've been thinking a lot and patiently waiting
Here's an interesting point of view, I'm shaking
You've redefined my definition of breathtaking
You've got a very unique way of vibrating

Waiting

She knows that I will still be waiting
For her never leaving which is creating
The most intense sensations it's frustrating
Not see my love but there's no debating
Some people and things are worth waiting
For she calls me baby but we're not dating
I'm coaching her and hydrating
My bitch she is the most fascinating
Thing on this planet she's skating
Often if she could I started activating
Her inner whore now I'm creating
Deeper, darker desires by alternating
Between sweet and disgusting her hips are rotating
She's gagging for my dick, she's tired of waiting
She'll do anything especially humiliating
To avoid his cold and stern berating
She focuses and he keeps her concentrating
On being her very best I'm dominating
My bitch is what she's always craving
She misses me and is eagerly waiting

WAKE

I think about you while dreaming and when I wake
I think of you in only an apron ad you bake
Me delicious food and sit on my lap and shake
Your hot hips whispering in you ear to make
You wake up hornier and hotter let me wake
Up your inner pervert it was fate
That brought us together I like to break
Your hot ass wide open feeding you cake
Smothering you, flattening you like a pancake
My big ass in your face making you shake
With pleasure I make you as wet as a lake
I dream of being with you as I take
Your breath away choking you when you're awake
You bring out the beast on me, you really wake
Up my passion her juices on a cupcake
I dream off you all night into the daybreak
You make me feel alive, like an earthquake
I can tell dreaming of you is impossible to fake
This large erection you cause when I wake

Wallpaper

She started using my poetry as wallpaper
Which inspires me to start to be greater
I will share with her the fruits of my labor
Happily and bravely I add another layer
Whispering the most loving prayer
Let my words make the most beautiful wallpaper
Writing passionately, unable to wait for later
She sings my words like a record player
She's surrounded by motivating wallpaper

Writer

She moaned that I was her favorite writer
I make her pussy turn into a hungry tiger
As my hands around her throat grow tighter
How dirty I make her feel so much desire
I bring out the filthiest in her, best erotic writer
Bruising her ass smacking her feel so much fire
Dripping on the floor she loves how I inspire
Her to be the nastiest whore every fiber
Of her being is drenched I stick my lighter
In her mouth and soon a whole crew of firefighters
Surround her spraying their milk makes her hyper
Stretching her holes and her mind wider
She loves being stretched by the dirtiest writer

www.ingramcontent.com/pod-product-compliance
Lightning Source LLC
Chambersburg PA
CBHW070852050426
42453CB00012B/2159